P9-CDE-632

Can I tell you about Dyslexia?

BOOK SOLD
NO LONGER R H PL
PROPERTY

Can I tell you about...?

The "Can I tell you about...?" series offers simple introductions to a range of limiting conditions. Friendly characters invite readers to learn about their experiences of living with a particular condition and how they would like to be helped and supported. These books serve as excellent starting points for family and classroom discussions.

Other subjects covered in the "Can I tell you about...?" series

ADHD

Asperger Syndrome

Asthma

Dementia

Epilepsy

OCD

Parkinson's Disease

Selective Mutism

Stuttering/Stammering

Can I tell you about Dyslexia?

A guide for friends, family and professionals

ALAN M. HULTQUIST
Illustrated by Bill Tulp

Jessica Kingsley *Publishers*
London and Philadelphia

First published in 2013
by Jessica Kingsley Publishers
116 Pentonville Road
London N1 9JB, UK
and
400 Market Street, Suite 400
Philadelphia, PA 19106, USA

www.jkp.com

Copyright © Alan M. Hultquist 2013
Illustrations copyright © Bill Tulp 2013

All rights reserved. No part of this publication may be reproduced in
any material form (including photocopying or storing it in any medium
by electronic means and whether or not transiently or incidentally to
some other use of this publication) without the written permission of the
copyright owner except in accordance with the provisions of the Copyright,
Designs and Patents Act 1988 or under the terms of a licence issued by the
Copyright Licensing Agency Ltd, Saffron House, 6–10 Kirby Street, London
EC1N 8TS. Applications for the copyright owner's written permission to
reproduce any part of this publication should be addressed to the publisher.

Warning: The doing of an unauthorised act in relation to a copyright work
may result in both a civil claim for damages and criminal prosecution.

Library of Congress Cataloging in Publication Data
Hultquist, Alan M.
Can I tell you about dyslexia? : a guide for friends,
family, and professionals / Alan M. Hultquist ;
illustrated by Bill Tulp.
pages cm
Audience: 7+
ISBN 978-1-84905-952-7 (alk. paper)
1. Dyslexic children--Juvenile literature. 2. Dyslexic
children. 3. Dyslexia. 4. Dyslexia--Juvenile
literature. I. Tulp, Bill, illustrator. II. Title.
RJ496.A5H845 2013
618.92'8553--dc23
2013010991

British Library Cataloguing in Publication Data
A CIP catalogue record for this book is available from the British Library.

ISBN 978 1 84905 952 7
eISBN 978 0 85700 810 7

Printed and bound in Great Britain by Bell & Bain Ltd, Glasgow

RICHMOND HILL PUBLIC LIBRARY
32972000198418 OR
Can I tell you about dyslexia? : a guide
Jan. 19, 2017

I dedicate this book to MK.

Acknowledgements

Many people were involved either directly or indirectly with the creation of this book, starting with my parents, Alma B. Ekstrom and Everett A. Hultquist. Their support started me down my career path. Lorna Murphy taught me about the nature of learning difficulties, including dyslexia. During the 33 years of my career, I got valuable insights from students, colleagues and parents. Lucy Buckroyd, at Jessica Kingsley Publishers, suggested I write this book. RSK, KL, Ginette Perry, Sandy Sherburne and AS offered comments about one or more drafts. And Robin Stander tried to make sure my final draft was better than my earlier ones. I apologise to anyone I might have forgotten.

I am deeply appreciative of the support and help provided by my husband, Brendan Hadash. For many different reasons, this book would not exist without him.

Finally, although people offered comments and suggestions about the manuscript, the responsibility for the final content, including any errors or omissions, is entirely mine.

Contents

"I'd like to tell you what it's like, what it feels like and how you might help me."

"You can't tell that I have dyslexia by looking at me. I look like most other girls. But you might notice some things about me that are a bit different. This is because dyslexia can make it harder for me to learn. Like everyone else, people with dyslexia are individuals, and it affects each person a bit differently. So, other people with dyslexia will be like me in some ways, but not in others.

Because of my dyslexia, I have trouble with some things that don't give most people a hard time. My main problems are with reading, spelling, writing down my thoughts, figuring out arithmetic answers and remembering words. But there are also things I'm really good at, like art and music. And I learn well when people show me what to do."

"Learning to understand the alphabet was hard for me."

"Most kids learn the alphabet without too much trouble. The teacher tells them the names of the letters and what sounds they make. After the children practise for a while, they remember them. But the alphabet confused me.

I understood that b, d, p and q were all different letters. But I had a hard time remembering which was which because they look so much alike. Sometimes, I can still mix these letters up in my writing if I don't stop to think about them first.

I also had trouble remembering letter sounds because they didn't always make sense. Some letters make two different sounds, and sometimes two or more letters make the same sound. This was confusing. Some of the letter names helped me, but others were a puzzle, like the letter y. It starts with a w sound, but that's not what it says when you read. The vowels (the letters a, e, i, o and u) were even more confusing because they make so many different sounds. I understand them a little better now."

"I'm still learning how to work with the sounds in words."

"Last year, the other kids in my class could tell the teacher what sound was at the beginning of a word, and even what sound was in the middle. But I didn't understand what they were doing because I couldn't separate the sounds in words. For me, words were just one sound. For example, I couldn't tell that the word *dog* had separate sounds for *d, o* and *g*. It just seemed like one big sound.

I needed lots of extra help before I understood that words are made of smaller sounds and that I can use those sounds to help me read. After I learned that, written words started to make more sense.

I still have some trouble working with the sounds in words. I can't always tell how many sounds there are or what order they're in. So I practise with my reading teacher every day. He has me take words apart into their separate sounds and blend sounds together to make words. He also has me change a specific sound in a word to a different one in order to create a new word. "

"I have trouble figuring out new words. But even when I *can* read them, it takes a lot of practice before I remember them."

"The other kids in my class seem to read new words without much trouble. I can figure out *some* words on my own, but it takes a lot of effort and I often need help. I can't always tell from the letters how many sounds are in a word, and I sometimes get confused when the letters and sounds don't match.

After most kids read a word five or six times, they know it forever. Remembering new words is a lot harder for me. I might have to read a word a hundred times before I really know it.

I work with my reading teacher every day. He teaches me how to know when a group of letters will make just one sound. He also teaches me rules so I know when a letter will make a specific sound. And we read lots of books together."

"Sometimes I forget words that I know really well."

"Even when I know the words, reading can *still* be frustrating. I might read a word perfectly, but have a hard time recalling it a few sentences later. I know the word, but I have trouble finding it quickly in my memory. So I might pause for a bit before reading it. Or I might keep reading, but accidentally say a word that looks a lot like the one on the page. For example, I might accidentally read *chicken* as *children*.

I can also have trouble remembering words when I'm talking. I know what I want to say, but sometimes I just can't think of the right words. So I have to stop and try to find them in my memory. I do often find the words I want, but sometimes I can't. When that happens, I end up using unclear words like *thing* and *stuff*. It helps if an adult gives me the first sound or syllable of the word I want. That's usually all I need to help me remember it. My speech teacher is helping me get better at finding the right words on my own."

"I almost always read slowly."

"Sometimes, I don't read very fast because I have to stop to figure words out. Other times, I read slowly because I have to reread words or sentences before I can understand them. But even when I know all the words and understand all the sentences, I still read more slowly than my friends do. I'm often the last one to finish in class and sometimes I don't even have enough time to read everything.

If my homework involves a lot of reading, my parents and older sister help me out. I read one page of a book, and one of them reads the next page.

I spend time every night practising how to read better. My parents give me a paragraph or page to read aloud. First, they make sure I really know all the words. Then, they read it to me so I'll know how it should sound. Next, they time me as I read the text to them. Then I read it a few more times and try to beat my speed each time. But I also try to use good phrasing and expression because good reading isn't just about being fast."

"Reading seems to be so much easier for the other kids than it is for me."

"When I think about how my friends read, I get a picture in my mind of them running down a road made of words. The teacher tells them to start, and they take off and run the whole way without any trouble. The words make a nice, flat surface for them to run on. And the sky is clear so they know exactly where they're going. When they get to the end, they can look back and see the whole road.

But when I think about how I read, I get a different picture in my mind. I'm trying to run on the same road, but the words don't make a completely flat surface. Some of the words and letters stick up and I trip over them. Other words are as big as boulders that I have to climb over. And it's often foggy, so I have to go slowly, even when parts of the road are smooth. When I get to the end, I'm tired. And when I look back, I can't see where I started. So I feel lost and can't remember what the words were."

"Reading is hard, but
spelling is even harder."

"I study really hard for my spelling tests and do my best to get the words right. But after a few days, I sometimes forget how to spell them.

I try to spell words the way they sound, but I can mix up some sounds and leave out others. Sometimes I have the right sounds, but use the wrong letters. Silent letters give me a hard time too. I might write them in the wrong order or forget to include them.

I *can* spell many words correctly, and I'm learning new ones all the time. I have some special ways of studying that help. When I practise words, I say the letters aloud as I write them. And if there are tricky parts in a word, I write them in colour to help me remember what they are. Also, my teacher is helping me learn some spelling rules that let me know which letters to use. So I'm working hard and my spelling is always getting better."

"Spelling isn't the only hard part about writing. It's also hard for me to put my ideas on paper."

"When I need to write a story or answer questions, I usually know what I want to say. But when I start to write, my thoughts get mixed up and I can't think of the right words.

My trouble with spelling also messes up my writing. If I try really hard to spell words correctly, I forget what I want to write. If there are words I know I won't be able to spell, I try to use other ones that I *can* spell. But then I don't write exactly what I want. And sometimes I focus so much on writing the words that I forget to use capital letters and punctuation. When I'm done, I feel frustrated because what's on the paper is never as good as the thoughts I had in my head.

Talking with an adult before I start writing helps. They make notes to remind me of what I want to say and what words I want to use. And sometimes I get to talk into a computer that types the words as I say them. I really like that!"

"I don't have trouble understanding most mathematical ideas, but I do have a hard time with other parts of mathematics."

"It took me longer than the other kids to learn the numbers. Regular counting and skip counting were both hard, and I wrote some numbers backwards. I still sometimes put numbers in the wrong order, like writing 63 when I mean 36.

I also have trouble remembering number facts, so I use my fingers a lot when I figure out answers. That means I need more time to do the work than the other kids do. And sometimes I get an answer incorrect because I counted wrong. It's great when the teacher lets me use a calculator!

I can have a hard time answering problem-solving questions if I need to read them by myself. I understand the stories better when someone reads them with me and I draw pictures to show what's happening."

"Sometimes I have trouble following and remembering directions."

"Most of the time, I don't have any trouble understanding what people say, but I find some direction words hard. Words like *before*, *across*, *right* and *left* always used to give me trouble. I'm better with them now, but sometimes I still get mixed up. And I often have to stop and think about which is my right side and which is my left.

I find long directions hard to follow. If my parents say, 'Zoe, brush your teeth, pick up your toys and make sure your homework is in your backpack before you go to bed', I can only remember to do part of it. When the teacher gives us long directions at school, I often watch what the other kids are doing so I can follow along. And sometimes I ask the teacher to repeat what she said.

I remember better if people tell me to do just one or two things at a time. It also helps if adults write down what I need to do. Then, if I forget, I can look at the list."

"Even though some schoolwork
is hard for me, there are lots
of things I'm really good at."

"I learn well when people show me what to do.

Just like my sister, I'm good at dancing and playing the violin. We take lessons together.

I'm very creative and I have a great imagination. I'm also good at thinking in pictures. So I'm really good at art, making things with my hands and fixing stuff. Whenever I have time, I help my father repair small engines in his workshop. He says that if I want to, I could be a mechanic when I'm older. But I think I'd rather be an artist or a dancer, or maybe even a doctor like my mother.

I'm in a children's acting group. I need to work hard to memorise my lines, but after we put on a play, everyone tells me that I'm a good actor.

And I'm really good at making people laugh."

"I know I have dyslexia
because my parents took me
to a learning specialist."

"A special kind of psychologist gave me some tests. I did some reading, writing and mathematics. I answered a bunch of questions and copied some designs. And I solved lots of different puzzles. It was hard work, but he made it fun.

The psychologist told us I'm smart, but some of the reading parts of my brain work a little differently to how they're supposed to. That's why I have trouble. I was really happy to hear that I'm smart! I hoped I was, but some parts of school were so hard for me that I felt kind of stupid.

He also said that *everyone* is good at some things, but finds other things difficult. So I'm just like everyone else. I was happy to hear that too!

The psychologist told us that dyslexia doesn't go away, but there are ways teachers can help. I was disappointed to find out that I'll always have dyslexia. But I'm ready to try hard and do my best."

How teachers can help

"The people at school help me a lot. They know students with dyslexia need a different kind of teaching to become good readers and spellers. So I work with a special teacher during part of every day. But *all* the teachers do things to help me. Here are some of the things they do."

GENERAL IDEAS

- "My teachers, parents and I work as a team to help me be successful.

- The teachers are patient. They know I'm doing my best and understand how hard I'm working.

- My teachers know that I read, spell and remember a little better on some days than others. They understand this is part of how my brain works and that on one day I might be able to do something that the next day I forget how to do.

- Teachers don't let other students see my work unless they ask me first. They understand I can feel embarrassed about my poor spelling and handwriting.

- The teachers let me take special classes and join after-school activities, like cooking, art and sports. They know I need the chance to be successful at things I enjoy.

- Some of my teachers wanted to hold me back because of my school difficulties. But after the psychologist talked with them, they understood that repeating a year/grade wouldn't fix my learning problems."

TEACHING

- "My teachers make learning as visual and hands-on as possible. They don't just tell me what they mean; they show me. And they give me visual reminders.

- The teachers also use *think aloud* procedures and *explicit instruction* to make their lessons more understandable.

- Teachers keep their verbal directions short. Sometimes, they check with me quietly, after they've given directions to the class, to make sure I'm ready to work on my own.

- My teachers understand that it can take me longer than the other students to do some work. So they give me extra time or only grade the parts I complete.

- The teachers make sure I get extra time to complete important tests. And, when it's appropriate, they let an adult write down my answers and help me read some of the words.

- Teachers don't put me on the spot when they ask questions. Instead, they direct questions to the entire class, provide time for everyone to think and then ask for answers."

READING

- "My teachers make sure the books and papers I have to read are available for me to listen to in case I need it. And they make sure there's an adult ready to help if I get stuck and only need a little support.

- When they make tests and worksheets, the teachers use a good-sized, sans serif font and double-spaced paragraphs. They also make sure the computer puts a little extra space between letters. They know the extra lines and spaces make it a bit easier for me to read.

- The teachers call on me when I volunteer to read aloud in class, but they don't ask me to read in front of my classmates without any warning. If teachers do expect me to read aloud, they tell me the day before exactly what sentences I should practise."

WRITING

- "My teachers let me to do homework on our home computer, and they sometimes say it's okay if I tell the answers to my parents so they can write them down.

- The teachers let me do some oral reports or projects instead of always having to do a lot of writing.

- If the teachers can't understand what I wrote, they ask me privately to read it to them and give me a chance to explain what I meant.

- Teachers don't make me do a lot of copying. But when I do need to copy something, they check with me privately to make sure I got it right."

MATHEMATICS

- "After I can show them that I understand how to do the work, teachers let me use a calculator or a number chart to find the answers. But they also work with me to help me get better at remembering and figuring out number facts.

- The teachers take time to explain how different words and phrases can mean the same thing (like *in all* and *all together*, *multiplication* and *times*, or *goes into* and *divided by*).

- If I'm having trouble learning a new skill, the teachers break it down into smaller steps so they can find out what part I need to work on.

- Teachers use the C–R–A sequence when they introduce a new skill. They begin instruction at the *concrete* level by using hands-on materials. Then they move to the *representational* level by using things like pictures and tallies. And then they help me transfer what I learned to the *abstract* level of just written numbers and mathematical symbols.

- The teachers also help me understand mathematical ideas by using colour-coding, finding ways to help me walk and talk myself through procedures, and by showing me how skills relate directly to my life.

- Teachers help me understand mathematical problem-solving stories by using *schema-based instruction*."

How parents can help

"My parents do a lot to help me too."

AT SCHOOL

- "My parents found out as much as they could about dyslexia and special education. Now they work with my teachers to make sure I'm getting what I need, both at school and at home.

- My parents talked with my teachers and they all agreed I could use a spelling flow list instead of taking a weekly spelling test: I get a few words to learn at a time and take a daily test on them. When I can spell a word correctly three days in a row, the teacher sets it aside and puts a new word on the list. But if I forget how to spell a word, the teacher puts it back on the flow list so I can study it again.

- My parents talk with all my teachers about the kinds of assistive technology I might need, like recorded books, an electronic dictionary, a tablet computer, different kinds of apps and voice recognition software."

AT HOME

- "My parents and I set up a separate, quiet area for me to do homework.

- It used to take me twice as long as the other students to do my homework. Now, my parents ask my teachers how long it takes the average student to do each homework assignment. Then they let me work on it for only that amount of time. But they make sure I'm working the whole time.

- My parents read with me every night. They don't let me struggle on a word for more than four seconds. If I can't figure it out, they tell me what it is.

- They also read age-appropriate books to me and get me recorded books that I can listen to on my own.

- It helped a lot when my parents and the psychologist talked with me about why I was having trouble at school. They waited until I was ready before we had that talk. And they told me it's okay if I want to talk with a counsellor about my learning problems.

- My parents are really positive and focus on the things I *can* do. They know I struggle with some parts of school, but they don't give me a hard time about it. They know I'm working hard to do my best."

Possible early signs of dyslexia

Here are some possible signs that *might* indicate a preschool or kindergarten-aged child is at risk of developing dyslexia.

- A family history of reading problems.

- Learning how to talk later than usual.

- Speech that's hard to understand.

- Mixing up the order of sounds in words (like saying *aminal* for *animal*).

- Trouble rhyming and playing with word sounds.

- Difficulty using blocks or other objects to show the number of words in sentences or the number of syllables in words.

- Trouble following oral directions.

- Difficulty understanding directional words (such as *front*, *behind*, *top*, *after*).

- Problems recalling the names of people or things.

- Trouble memorising sequences, like the counting numbers, months, days of the week, and the alphabet.

Dyslexia doesn't go away, but with the right teaching, many children make a lot of progress. The earlier children get help, the more progress they're likely to make. So, if a young child shows more than the average amount of trouble with three or more of the skills listed on the previous page, it's probably a good idea to ask for an evaluation.

Some important ideas to know

These are some of the processing skills that can make school hard for students with dyslexia.

PHONEMIC AWARENESS

This is the understanding that *spoken* words are made up of individual sounds.

Students with a phonemic awareness problem have a hard time separating words into sounds, isolating individual sounds in words, counting the number of sounds in words and manipulating those sounds. They struggle to sound out words. When they spell, they tend to leave out sounds, get sounds in the wrong order and use the wrong sounds. Children who struggle with phonemic awareness will most likely show it before starting school. They'll probably have three or more of the early signs of dyslexia mentioned in the last section.

Phonemic awareness is important because it helps children understand phonics, which is the connection between the sounds in words and the printed letters.

ORTHOGRAPHIC AWARENESS

This refers to understanding the *written* parts of language, such as numerals, letters and spelling patterns.

Students with an orthographic awareness problem are often good at sounding out words that follow the letter–sound rules, but struggle with words that don't closely follow those rules. When they read, these students tend to make mistakes on function words (such as *the*, *while* and *of*) and word endings (such as *-ly*, *-ed* and *-s*). Their spelling often has all the right sounds, but the wrong letters; and silent letters may be missing or in the wrong order. Students who struggle with orthographic awareness have a hard time with homophones, confuse *b* and *d* long after their peers have mastered them, and sometimes have more than one way of misspelling words. They might also write digits backward or put numerals in the wrong order.

RAPID AUTOMATISED (OR AUTOMATIC) NAMING (RAN)

This is the ability to quickly and consistently name rows of simple objects, such as coloured squares or letters.

Students with a RAN problem will name these objects slowly or inconsistently. And since they can't read letters quickly, they also don't read words rapidly. Instead, their reading is slow and they sometimes read a word correctly in one sentence, but then don't recall the same word a few sentences later.

Any student with a reading problem can be a slow reader, but it's not always because of a rapid naming problem. So, if a student reads slowly, it's important to find out why.

WORKING MEMORY

This refers to how much information a person can actively keep "in the back of their head" and work with at the same time.

If a student's working memory capacity isn't large enough, they won't be able to mentally hold on to all the information needed to get the job done.

A weak working memory can affect just about any part of school. Students with a working memory problem might be able to tell you all the sounds in a word, but be unable to put those sounds together to read the word. They might be able to read all the words in a chapter, but not remember what the chapter is about. They might spell words correctly on a dictated test, but misspell those same words when they're writing. And they might not be able to remember multi-step directions or do arithmetic in their head.

Recommended reading, organisations and websites

BOOKS FOR CHILDREN AND TEENS

Hale, N. (2004) *Oh Brother! Growing up with a Special Needs Sibling*. Washington, DC: Magination Press.

Hallowell, E.M. (2004) *A Walk in the Rain with a Brain*. New York: HarperCollins.

Hultquist, A.M. (2008) *What is Dyslexia? A Book Explaining Dyslexia for Kids and Adults to Use Together*. London: Jessica Kingsley Publishers.

Stern, J.M. and Ben-Ami, U. (2010) *Many Ways to Learn: A Kid's Guide to LD* (second edition). Washington, DC: Magination Press.

BOOKS FOR PARENTS

Cooper-Kahn, J. and Dietzel, L. (2008) *Late, Lost, and Unprepared: A Parents' Guide to Helping Children with Executive Functioning*. Bethesda, MD: Woodbine House.

Dawson, P. and Guare, R. (2009) *Smart but Scattered: The Revolutionary Executive Skills Approach to Helping Kids Reach Their Potential*. New York: Guilford Press.

Guare, R., Dawson, P. and Guare, C. (2013) *Smart but Scattered Teens: The Executive Skills Program for Helping Teens Reach Their Potential*. New York: Guilford Press.

Hultquist, A.M. (2006) *An Introduction to Dyslexia for Parents and Professionals*. London: Jessica Kingsley Publishers.

Hultquist, A.M. (2008) *What is Dyslexia? A Book Explaining Dyslexia for Kids and Adults to Use Together*. London: Jessica Kingsley Publishers.

Reid, G. (2011) *Dyslexia: A Complete Guide for Parents and Those Who Help Them* (second edition). Chichester: John Wiley & Sons.

Stein, J., Meltzer, L., Krishnan, K., Pollica, L.S., Papadopoulos, I. and Roditi, B. (2007) *Parent Guide to Hassle-Free Homework: Proven Practices that Work from the Research Institute for Learning and Development*. New York: Scholastic Teaching Resources.

Shaywitz, S. (2003) *Overcoming Dyslexia: A New and Complete Science-Based Program for Reading Problems at Any Level*. New York: Alfred A. Knopf.

BOOKS FOR PROFESSIONALS
General information about reading, mathematics and dyslexia

Berch, D.B. and Mazzocco, M.M.M. (2007) *Why is Math So Hard for Some Children? The Nature and Origins of Mathematical Learning Difficulties and Disabilities*. Baltimore, MD: Paul H. Brookes Publishing.

Dowker, A. (2005) *Individual Differences in Arithmetic: Implications for Psychology, Neuroscience and Education*. Brighton: Psychology Press.

Hannell, G. (2004) *Dyslexia: Action Plans for Successful Learning*. London: David Fulton Publishers.

Hannell, G. (2013) *Dyscalculia: Action Plans for Successful Learning in Mathematics* (second edition). Oxford: Routledge.

Hultquist, A.M. (2006) *An Introduction to Dyslexia for Parents and Professionals.* London: Jessica Kingsley Publishers.

Mather, N. and Wendling, B.J. (2012) *Essentials of Dyslexia Assessment and Intervention.* Hoboken, NJ: Wiley & Sons.

Reid, G. (2009) *Dyslexia: A Practitioner's Handbook* (fourth edition). Chichester: John Wiley & Sons.

Shaywitz, S. (2003) *Overcoming Dyslexia: A New and Complete Science-Based Program for Reading Problems at Any Level.* New York: Alfred A. Knopf.

Wolf, M. (2007) *Proust and the Squid: The Story and Science of the Reading Brain.* New York: HarperCollins.

General teaching and school-based interventions

Archer, A.L. and Hughes, C.A. (2011) *Explicit Instruction: Effective and Efficient Teaching.* New York: Guilford Press.

Hollingsworth, J. and Ybarra, S. (2009) *Explicit Direct Instruction: The Power of the Well-Crafted, Well-Taught Lesson.* Thousand Oaks, CA: Corwin Press.

Rathvon, N. (2008) *Effective School Interventions* (second edition). New York: Guilford Press.

Wendling, B.J. and Mather, N. (2009) *Essentials of Evidence-Based Academic Interventions.* Hoboken, NJ: Wiley & Sons.

Teaching phonemic awareness

Adams, M.J., Footman, B.R., Lundberg, I. and Beeler, T. (1998) *Phonemic Awareness in Young Children: A Classroom Curriculum.* Baltimore, MD: Paul H. Brookes Publishing.

Blachman, B.A., Ball, E.W., Black, R. and Tangel, D.M. (2000) *Road to the Code: A Phonological Awareness Program for Young Children.* Baltimore, MD: Paul H. Brookes Publishing.

Richards, R.G. (1999) *The Source for Dyslexia and Dysgraphia.* East Moline, IL: LinguiSystems.

Teaching reading and spelling

Bear, D.R., Invernizzi, M.R., Templeton, S. and Johnston, F.R. (2011) *Words Their Way: Word Study for Phonics, Vocabulary, and Spelling Instruction* (fifth edition). Upper Saddle River, NJ: Pearson.

Birsh, J.R. (ed.) (2011) *Multisensory Teaching of Basic Language Skills* (third edition). Baltimore, MD: Paul H. Brookes Publishing.

Bluedorn, H. (2004) *Handy English Encoder Decoder: All the Spelling and Phonics Rules You Could Ever Want to Know* (second edition). New Boston, IL: Trivium Pursuit.

Caldwell, J.S. and Leslie, L. (2012) *Intervention Strategies to Follow Informal Reading Inventory Assessment: So What Do I Do Now?* (third edition) Boston, MA: Pearson.

Henry, M.K. (2010) *Unlocking Literacy: Effective Decoding and Spelling Instruction* (second edition). Baltimore, MD: Paul H. Brookes Publishing.

McKenna, M.C. (2002) *Help for Struggling Readers: Strategies for Grades 3–8.* New York: Guilford Press.

Swigert, N.B. (2003) *The Source for Reading Fluency.* East Moline, IL: LinguiSystems.

Teaching writing

Harris, K.R., Graham, S., Mason, L.H. and Friedlander, B. (2007) *Powerful Writing Strategies for All Students*. Baltimore: Paul H. Brookes Publishing.

Mather, N., Wendling, B.J. and Roberts, R. (2009) *Writing Assessment and Instruction for Students with Learning Disabilities*. San Francisco, CA: Jossey-Bass.

Teaching mathematics

Bley, N.S. and Thorton, C.A. (2001) *Teaching Mathematics to Students with Learning Disabilities*. Austin, TX: Pro-Ed.

Fuchs, L.S., Seethaler, P.M., Powell, S.R. and Fuchs, D. (not dated) *Pirate Math: Let's Find X! A Tutoring Program for Remediating Difficulty with Word Problems*. Nashville, TN: Vanderbilt University.

Jitendra, A.K. (2007) *Solving Math Word Problems: Teaching Students with Learning Disabilities Using Schema-Based Instruction*. Austin, TX: Pro-Ed.

Montague, M. and Jitendra, A.K. (eds) (2006) *Teaching Mathematics to Middle School Students with Learning Difficulties*. New York: Guilford Press.

Memory, organisation, planning, attention and other executive functions

Dawson, P. and Guare, R. (2012) *Coaching Students with Executive Skills Deficits*. New York: Guilford Press.

Dawson, P. and Guare, R. (2010) *Executive Skills in Children and Adolescents: A Practical Guide to Assessment and Intervention*. New York: Guilford Press.

Dehn, M.J. (2008) *Working Memory and Academic Learning: Assessment and Intervention.* Hoboken, NJ: Wiley & Sons.

Dehn, M.J. (2010) *Long-Term Memory Problems in Children and Adolescents: Assessment, Intervention, and Effective Instruction.* Hoboken, NJ: Wiley & Sons.

Meltzer, L. (2010) *Promoting Executive Function in the Classroom.* New York: Guilford Press.

Richards, R.G. (2003) *The Source for Learning and Memory Strategies.* East Moline, IL: LinguiSystems.

INTERNATIONAL ORGANISATIONS AND WEBSITES

This information was correct at the time the book was written.

UK

British Dyslexia Association
Unit 8, Bracknell Beeches
Old Bracknell Lane
Bracknell
RG12 7BW
Phone: 0845 251 9002
Email: helpline@bdadyslexia.org.uk
Website: www.bdadyslexia.org.uk

Dyslexia Action
Park House
Wick Road
Egham
Surrey
TW20 0HH
Phone: 01784 222300
Email: via website
Website: http://dyslexiaaction.org.uk

Northern Ireland Dyslexia Association
17A Upper Newtownards Road
Belfast
BT4 3HT
Phone: 028 9065 9212
Email: via website
Website: www.nida.org.uk

Dyslexia Scotland
2nd floor – East Suite
Wallace House
17–21 Maxwell Place
Stirling
FK8 1JU
Phone: 0844 800 8484
Email: helpline@dyslexiascotland.org.uk
Website: www.dyslexiascotland.com

Dyslecsia Cymru/Wales Dyslexia
University of Wales Trinity St David
Carmarthen
SA31 3EP
Phone: 0808 1800 110
Email: via website
Website: www.walesdyslexia.org.uk

Miles Dyslexia Centre
Bangor University
Gwynedd
LL57 2DG
Phone: (01248) 382203
Email: dyslex-admin@bangor.ac.uk
Website: www.dyslexia.bangor.ac.uk

Republic of Ireland

Dyslexia Association of Ireland
Suffolk Chambers
1 Suffolk Street
Dublin 2
Phone: 01 6790276
Email: info@dyslexia.ie
Website: www.dyslexia.ie

USA

Council for Exceptional Children
2900 Crystal Drive, Suite 1000
Arlington, VA 22202–3557
Phone: 888 232 7733
Email: service@cec.sped.org (or via website)
Website: www.cec.sped.org

Council for Learning Disabilities
11184 Antioch Road
Box 405
Overland Park, KS 66210
Phone: 913 491 1011
Email: CLDInfo@cldinternational.org
Website: www.cldinternational.org

Learning Ally (for audio textbooks)
20 Roszel Road
Princeton, NJ 08540
Phone: 800 221 4792
Email: bvidialogue@LearningAlly.org
Website: via website

Learning Disabilities Association of America
4156 Library Road
Pittsburgh, PA 15234–1349
Phone: 412 341 1515
Email: via website
Website: www.ldanatl.org

International Dyslexia Association
40 York Road, 4th Floor
Baltimore, MD 21204
Phone: 410 296 0232
Email: via website
Website: www.interdys.org

Canada

Canadian Dyslexia Association
57, rue du Couvent
Gatineau, QC J9H 3C8
Phone: 613 853 6539
Email: info@dyslexiaassociation.ca
Website: www.dyslexiaassociation.ca

Learning Disabilities Association of Canada
2420 Bank Street, Suite 20
Ottawa, ON K1V 8S1
Phone: 613 238 5721
Email: info@ldac-acta.ca
Website: www.ldac-acta.ca

Australia

SPELD Australia (Supporting People with Learning Disabilities)
PO Box 409
South Perth, WA 6951
Phone: 08 9217 2500
Email: support@dsf.net.au
Website: www.auspeld.org.au

New Zealand

Dyslexia Foundation of New Zealand
PO Box 16141
Hornby
Christchurch
Phone: email preferred for all general enquiries
Email: info@dfnz.org.nz
Website: www.dyslexiafoundation.org.nz

Learning and Behaviour Charitable Trust
PO Box 40–161
Lower Hutt 5011
New Zealand
Phone: contact by email or via links on website
Email: lbctnz@slingshot.co.nz
Website: www.lbctnz.co.nz

SPELD NZ (Supporting People with Learning Disabilities)
PO Box 24–042
Royal Oak
Auckland 1345
Phone: 09 6240839
Email: info@dfnz.org.nz
Website: www.speld.org.nz